Birthdays
Around the World

Celebrating Birthdays in Brazil

by Cheryl L. Enderlein

Content Consultant

Jose Eugenio Figueiredo
Translation Consultant
Brazilian-American Cultural Institute

Hilltop Books

An Imprint of Franklin Watts
A Division of Grolier Publishing
New York   London   Hong Kong   Sydney
Danbury, Connecticut

Hilltop Books
http://publishing.grolier.com
Published simultaneously in Canada.
Printed in the United States of America.

Library of Congress Cataloging-in-Publication Data
Enderlein, Cheryl L.
    Celebrating birthdays in Brazil/by Cheryl L. Enderlein.
    p. cm--(Birthdays around the world)
    Includes bibliographical references (p. 23) and index.
    Summary: Discusses the parties, decorations, food, music, games, and presents
found at Brazilian birthday celebrations.
    ISBN 1-56065-760-X
    1. Birthdays--Juvenile literature. 2. Children's parties--Brazil--Juvenile literature.
3. Brazil--Social life and customs--Juvenile literature. [1. Birthdays. 2. Parties.
3. Brazil--Social life and customs.] I. Title. II. Series.
    GV1472.7.B5E523   1998
    394.2--dc21

                                                97-44680
                                                 CIP
                                                   AC

Editorial credits

Editor, Mark Drew; additional editing, Colleen Sexton; cover design, Timothy Halldin; photo research,
    Michelle L. Norstad

Photo credits

Abril Imagens/Carol Do Valle, 8; Antonio Rodrigues, 12
Renato de Aguiar, 16
Lupe Cunha, 18
H. Huntly Hersch, 6
International Stock/Paulo Fridman, 20
Material World/Stephanie Maze, cover
Unicorn Stock Photos/Jeff Greenberg, 4; Batt Johnson, 14
Cristina Zappa, 10

Table of Contents

Facts about Brazil

Brazil is a country in South America. It is the fifth largest nation in the world. Brazil is almost as big as the United States.

Brazil has big cities and large areas of farmland. The world's biggest rain forest covers northern Brazil. Rain forests grow in hot, wet parts of the world.

People from Brazil are called Brazilians. Brazilians come from seven ethnic groups. An ethnic group is people who share the same background. The ethnic groups in Brazil include Portuguese, Africans, Indians, and Italians. Spanish, German, and Japanese people also live in Brazil.

Brazilians speak Portuguese. This is the language of a country in Europe called Portugal. Brazil was once a colony of Portugal. A colony is an area controlled by another country.

Brazil has big cities like Rio de Janeiro.

What Is a Birthday?

A birthday is the day a person was born. Each year, people celebrate turning a year older. Celebrate means to do something fun on a special occasion.

It is a tradition to celebrate a person's birthday. A tradition is something people have done for many years. Sometimes Brazilians celebrate with family members. Sometimes they celebrate with friends. People in different countries celebrate in different ways.

Everyone in the world has a birthday. In Brazil, the traditional birthday greeting is feliz aniversário (fay-LEEZ ahn-ih-ver-SAHR-ee-oh). It means happy birthday in Portuguese.

Sometimes Brazilians celebrate their birthdays with friends.

Theme Parties

Many Brazilian birthday parties have a theme. A theme is a main subject. The theme of a birthday party might be sports or animals. The party could have a princess theme or a superhero theme.

A birthday person's family buys or makes decorations. The decorations match the party's theme. Some Brazilian stores sell party goods. The family can choose party themes at these stores.

The birthday person's family decorates one room for the party. The family covers a table with a tablecloth. The tablecloth matches the theme. A poster hangs on the wall behind the table. Balloons hang from the walls and ceiling. The room looks like a make-believe world.

Many Brazilian birthday parties have a theme.

Food and Treats

Families make special meals for birthday parties. The guests drink soda pop while the family cooks. Guests are people who come to the party. The guests eat salts, too. Salts are tiny pastries stuffed with meat. Pastries taste like pie crust.

Family members set food on a big table. They serve small pieces of steak on sticks. They serve hot dogs covered with tomato sauce. People eat the meats with rice and manioc (MAN-ee-ahk). Manioc is a root that grows in Brazil. It tastes like potatoes.

Sweets are a birthday tradition in Brazil. One favorite sweet is a chocolate ball covered with sprinkles. Another sweet is made of chocolate and coconut. The family puts trays filled with sweets on the table. Each guest receives a bag filled with some sweets. These bags are called party favors.

Sweets are a birthday tradition in Brazil.

Birthday Cake

Everyone eats birthday cake after the meal. The cake is decorated to match the theme. The cake also has candles. Some families use one candle for each year of age. Some families use a candle shaped like a number. The number is the same as the birthday person's age.

Guests stand around the table. The birthday person stands behind the cake. An adult lights the candles and turns off the lights. Everyone sings to the birthday person. They clap while they sing songs.

Brazilians sing the same happy birthday song sung in North America. They sing it in Portuguese. Then they sing another song about blowing out the candles.

The birthday person makes a wish and blows out the candles. Then the birthday person eats the first piece of cake.

The birthday cake is decorated to match the party theme.

Fun and Games

A birthday party in Brazil is fun. Families and friends get together. People talk and laugh. There is music. People dance whenever they feel like it. Children play games.

Sometimes Brazilian children play a game called cabra-cega (KAH-brah SAY-gah). Cabra-cega is like hide and seek. Brazilian children might also play soccer at a birthday party. The Portuguese name for soccer is futebol (fooch-BOL).

Some Brazilian families hire clowns to perform for the children. Clowns might tell jokes or make balloon animals. Other families hire magicians. Magicians may do card tricks or make things disappear.

Some Brazilian families hire clowns to perform for the children.

Presents

Guests bring presents to the birthday party. They choose things they think the birthday person will like. They might buy a doll or a ball. They might buy a coloring book and crayons. They wrap their presents in colorful paper.

Guests greet the birthday person when they arrive. Brazilians say feliz aniversário and give their presents. Giving a present is another way of saying happy birthday.

The birthday person opens presents during the party. The family puts the opened presents on the birthday person's bed. Later, guests go to the bedroom to see all the presents.

The birthday person opens presents during the party.

A Special Birthday

A birthday is always special. But a Brazilian girl's 15th birthday is her most important birthday. This is called a coming of age birthday. Turning 15 means the girl is grown up.

It is a tradition to have a special party for the girl. Brazilians call this special party baile da debutante (BYE-lay DAH day-boo-TAHN-shay). This is a party to present the girl to the community.

Family and friends come to the party. Grandparents, aunts, uncles, and cousins come to celebrate. Friends bring their families to the party, too.

The party takes place outdoors if it is a warm day. Everyone dresses up. People eat a big meal and fancy desserts. A band plays after the meal. The girl and her father dance the first dance alone. Then the guests dance.

Brazilians have a special party on a girl's 15th birthday.

Brazil's Birthday

September 7 is Independence Day in Brazil. Brazil became free from Portugal on this day in 1822. This makes September 7 Brazil's birthday. Brazilians celebrate this birthday every year.

The colors green and yellow are seen everywhere on Independence Day. These are the colors of the Brazilian flag. Flags decorate the streets. People raise the flag outside their houses. Brazilians wear green and yellow clothing, too.

Brazilians go to parades on Independence Day. Children and adults march in the parades. Marching bands play Brazilian music. They also play Brazil's national anthem. The name of Brazil's national anthem is "Hino Nacional Brasileiro" (EE-noh nah-see-oh-NAHL brah-zee-lee-EH-roo). Brazilians celebrate Independence Day because they are proud of their country.

Brazilians go to parades on Independence Day.

Hands On: Plan a Theme Party

Plan a theme party. Pick anything you like as a theme. For example, you might choose bugs, flowers, or sports. Make some invitations and decorations for your party.

What You Need

Paper

Crayons or markers

Small paper bags

Candy, gum, and small toys

Poster board

Tape

What You Do

1. Make party invitations. Start by folding a piece of paper in half. Decorate the front using crayons or markers. Draw something that matches your theme. Write the words Come to My Party on the inside. Write the time and day of your party, too.
2. Make party favor bags. Decorate the outside of the paper bags. Put candy, gum, or toys in the bags.
3. Make a birthday poster to hang on the wall. Draw a picture that matches your theme on the poster board. Tape the poster to the wall.
4. Give the invitations to your friends. Invite them to come to your party.

Words to Know

celebrate (SEHL-uh-brayt)—to do something fun on a special occasion

ethnic group (ETH-nik GROOP)—people who share the same background

guest (GEST)—a person who comes to a party

invite (in-VITE)—to ask people to come

manioc (MAN-ee-ahk)—a root grown in Brazil that tastes like potatoes

salts (SAWLTS)—tiny pastries stuffed with meat

theme (THEEM)—the main subject of a party

tradition (truh-DISH-uhn)—something people have done for many years

Read More

Dahl, Michael. *Brazil.* Countries of the World. Mankato, Minn.: Bridgestone Books, 1997.

Dawson, Zoë. *Brazil.* Austin, Tex.: Raintree Steck-Vaughn Publishers, 1995.

Feldman, Eve B. *Birthdays! Celebrating Life Around the World.* Mahwah, N.J.: BridgeWater Books, 1996.

Haskins, Jim and Kathleen Benson. *Count Your Way through Brazil.* Minneapolis: Carolrhoda Books, Inc., 1996.

Useful Addresses

**Brazilian-American
  Chamber of Commerce**
22 West 48th St. NW
Suite 404
New York, NY 10036-1886

**Brazilian-American
  Cultural Institute**
4103 Connecticut Ave. NW
Washington, DC 20008

Internet Sites

Brazilian Embassy, Washington, D.C.
http://www.brasil.emb.nw.dc.us
Kids Parties Connection
http://kidsparties.com

Index